WHAT EVERY

Mother

NEEDS TO KNOW

BRENDA HUNTER

MULTNOMAH BOOKS • SISTERS, OREGON

WHAT EVERY MOTHER NEEDS TO KNOW
published by Multnomah Books
a part of the Questar publishing family

© 1993 by Brenda Hunter, Ph.D.

International Standard Book Number 0-88070-607-4

Printed in the United States of America

Most Scripture quotations are from the New International Version
© 1973, 1984 by International Bible Society
used by permission of Zondervan Publishing House

Scripture quotations marked KJV are from the King James Version

95 96 97 98 99 00 01 — 10 9 8 7 6 5

PREFACE

I've written this book for mothers on the run. Over the past five years I've spent a lot of time with busy mothers, especially mothers of young children, who tell me they need daily doses of encouragement, yet they find little time for themselves. They have only brief moments to read, yet they yearn for support and encouragement in a culture that devalues mothering. To meet their need for affirmation in capsules, I've written this little book that distills much of what I've learned as a psychologist, wife, and mother.

This book offers insights into the many aspects of a mother's life: her relationships with her husband, her young children, her teenagers, her parents, her friends, and herself. During the time I've been writing, I've asked myself—and many mothers—"What does every mother need to know?" I've tried to capture the essentials, to put on paper what I wish I had read when I embarked on motherhood.

I applaud mothers' efforts to give their children a sense of emotional security in what has become a rough, tough world. From the vantage point of midlife, I know that what mothers are doing has enormous value to society. And I know that on-site mothering does one day end. Children do grow up, and if they have "grown well into themselves," a mother has deep and abiding feelings of fulfillment.

Finally, I have written this book because I have loved being a mother these twenty-six years. And, yes, I'd do it all over again.

Brenda Hunter, Ph.D.
Vienna, Virginia

1.

No one will ever look at you with such a worshipful
gaze as your one-year-old.

2.

"Truth, which is important to a scholar, has got to be concrete.
And there is nothing more concrete than dealing with
babies, burps and bottles, frogs and mud."

JEANE J. KIRKPATRICK,
on how the rearing of three sons prepared her for her post as UN ambassador

3.

Caring for your children
in your corner of the world is the most challenging, frustrating,
and rewarding WORK you will ever do.

4.

Your adolescent daughter may acquire a distaste
for you when she turns twelve or thirteen.
She will, however, regain her sanity and realize what a wonderful
woman you are about three weeks before she leaves
home for college.

BRENDA HUNTER

5.

Babies are born geniuses—
programmed to discover all they need to know
about their world.

6.

Children acquire many of their language skills
from conversations with their mothers. So as you answer a zillion
questions throughout the day, you are enlarging your child's
vocabulary and his world.

7.

Contrary to cultural notions,
not just anyone can care for your children.
Mothering requires much intelligence, commitment,
patience, and creativity. Realize that you are strategically
important to your children's lives.

8.

You are creating both a physical and psychological home
for your children. Although they will leave the physical home,
they will carry the psychological home inside them
as long as they live.

BRENDA HUNTER

9.
Although the culture devalues mothers,
God and your children don't.

10.
As mothers, we are giving our children
a legacy of memories, both positive and negative.
It is important that the positive outweigh the negative—
that we give them a positive sense of home rather than a deep,
abiding sense of homelessness. How can we ensure this?
By being physically and emotionally present
much of the time they are home.

11.

Your children *will* grow up some day,
and instead of leaving the house with a diaper bag
slung over your shoulder,
you will carry a smart black purse and a briefcase.

12.

If you choose to stay home with your children,
you need to develop other interests as they mature.
You can do this by working part-time,
having a home-based business, or finding a passion
that will further shape your life.

BRENDA HUNTER

13.

Your home, whether large or small,
is a university where your children are taking graduate courses
in sharing, love, fair play, life.

14.

Don't praise your daughter's beauty overmuch.
She may become self-conscious
and feel that prettiness is all she possesses.
Instead, stress character, compassion, kindness, intelligence,
and grace—qualities she can cultivate
over a lifetime.

15.

You will never become all that you were meant to be
unless you make God your most intimate friend.

16.

Teenagers today receive wildly contradictory messages
about sex and values from the culture—
"Go ahead. Try it." "Abstain." "Use a condom
or you'll die from AIDS."
As a mother, you have a unique opportunity
to teach your child the proper role of sex. And start when he is
young and still adores you and believes all you say.

BRENDA HUNTER

17.

As Deanne was homeschooling her children one day,
she read them the story of Adam and Eve from Genesis.
When she asked her four-year-old son Zach
how Eve was punished for her sin,
Zach said with a smile,
"She had to take care of children!"

18.

Your daughter will learn how to nurture
her future children as she receives love and care from you.
So give her hugs and kisses daily.

19.

You are the architect of intimacy for your sons and daughters.
They will learn to speak the language of the heart from you.

20.

Don't label your children. Labels can be self-fulfilling.
In my family, I had the brains and my sister the personality.
It was years before I discovered that I had social skills
and she, that she was intelligent.

BRENDA HUNTER

21.

Some days your toughest task
will be getting up in the morning.
Plan ahead for those hormonal blues.

22.

You can become a woman of excellence
right in your own home.
Here, in addition to caring for your family's needs,
you have the freedom to learn, grow,
and spend time doing good work—
whether it is writing a book or growing a garden.

23.

A man who has a loving relationship with his dad
stands on his father's shoulders to view the world.

24.

"Children who grow up with their fathers
do far better—emotionally, educationally, physically,
every way we can measure—than children who do not....
The simple truth is that fathers are irreplaceable
in shaping the competence and character of their children."

DAVID BLANKENHORN, PRESIDENT OF THE INSTITUTE FOR AMERICAN VALUES

BRENDA HUNTER

25.

As your son learns to communicate openly with you,
he practices for future conversations with his wife.

26.

Teach your son
to treat each woman he dates
as a future wife for some fortunate man.
That way he will not exploit women sexually,
and as he treats women well,
he may become greathearted in the process.

27.

"You don't have to suffer to be a poet.
Adolescence is enough suffering for anyone."

JOHN CIARDI, POET

28.

Our children need our continuing presence
in their lives. Most agree that babies need mothers,
but teenagers also need mothers around.
Too many key decisions are made during adolescence:
whether to take drugs, engage in premarital sex,
or strive for academic excellence.

BRENDA HUNTER

29.

"Children are an heritage of the LORD."

PSALM 127:3, KJV

30.

When your kids are young,
it's hard to evaluate how you're doing.
No one issues report cards.
No boss gives you a periodic evaluation.
But if your child is flourishing and has a warm,
open, affectionate relationship with you,
you get an "A" in mothering.

31.

The very best gift you and your husband can give
your children is the privilege of growing up in a home
where the adults are wild about each other.

32.

Your husband picks up on your mood
four seconds after coming home each night.
If you are warm and cheerful,
you'll feel better and he will, too.

BRENDA HUNTER

33.

The federal government and the school
cannot possibly rear your children.
There isn't enough money in the federal budget
to pay people to be crazy about your kids.

34.

Kids need to know that the two most important people
in the world—their parents—love them dearly
and will make enormous sacrifices for their welfare.
If they feel this, they are far less likely to experience
the feelings of worthlessness and depression that lead to suicide.

35.

In the turbulent world we live in,
values are what keep our families together and sane.
Teach your kids to love God,
show compassion to others,
obey societal rules, and respect their own bodies.

36.

If you establish a close emotional bond
with your daughter when she is an infant,
then, when she is an adolescent,
your views on premarital sex will matter to her greatly.

BRENDA HUNTER

37.

Take time for special moments with your children.
My daughters are now young women,
involved in their careers and friendships,
yet among their fondest childhood memories
are teatimes spent at Olive's East, a small tearoom in Seattle.
And I fondly remember their ecstatic faces
as they divided a pastry and sipped juice.

38.

"I never thought that you should be rewarded
for the greatest privilege of life."

MAY ROPER COKER,
on being chosen Mother of the Year, 1958

39.

Never yell at your children in front of company
no matter how much they deserve it.

(Added, as penance, at the request of my daughter, Holly)

40.

Making a house into a home
inevitably involves some drudgery
and lots of personal discipline,
but the results are worth it.
Anyone can feel the difference
between a way station and a home.

BRENDA HUNTER

41.

You need an hour each day
to cultivate your inner life—your mind,
your spirit, your soul.

42.

You can nurture yourself
even if your emotional needs weren't met in childhood.
How? Spend time with a friend,
read a book of poetry, buy a geranium, get a facial.
Tell God your father that you need for him to show you, today,
that he loves you.

43.

Marriage, like wine, improves with age,
provided the ingredients are right.

44.

In most marriages
the first thirteen years are the hardest.
Around that time, you begin to accept the fact
that the man you married is not whom you envisioned.
Instead of blaming your partner for being himself,
use this time to really work on your marriage.

BRENDA HUNTER

45.

Your husband can never meet all of your emotional needs.
Poor man, he doesn't have your hormones.
You will always need the communion of other women.

46.

It may take years to turn your husband
into your confidant and best friend,
but it is well worth the effort.
Although he may not show it, he needs to feel close to you
nearly as much as you need to feel close to him.

47.

The roots of our low self-esteem can often be found
in our early relationships with our parents.
When we were young, we developed attitudes toward ourselves
based on the way our parents treated us.
Can we find healing?
Yes. In fact, caring for our children is one way
to overcome our pain and to bolster their self-esteem.

48.

To be truly oneself is to be an original.

BRENDA HUNTER

49.

"Infancy is a special time for mothers.
They have hormonal tools and distinct
psychological advantages which allow them
to more easily read and satisfy a newborn baby....
The critical period for the father begins
when the child starts to interact with the impersonal world."

KARL ZINSMEISTER, AUTHOR

50.

To your children,
you are the sun and your husband is the moon.

51.

Current media images of mothering are greatly distorted.
Any mother who puts her family first
will have to deflect much that she sees, hears, and reads.

52.

A woman is not washed up professionally
if she takes a season of her life to care for her children.
Sandra Day O'Connor, Supreme Court justice,
stayed home when her children were small,
as did former U.S. ambassador to the United Nations,
Jeane Kirkpatrick.

BRENDA HUNTER

53.

Your mother will take on new significance for you
the day you become a mother.
Within the first few days after your baby is born,
you will understand more about her than you have in years,
regardless of whether the relationship is positive or negative.
If possible, view her as an ally and enlist her aid.
It will help you care more effectively for your baby.

54.

"The virtues of mothers shall be visited upon their children."
CHARLES DICKENS

55.

Contrary to how you may feel as you care for preschoolers,
your brain is not rotting.
As your kids mature, you will discover—magically—
that your ability to think two consecutive thoughts returns.

56.

If you want to teach your child a task,
first show him how to do it and
then patiently work with him until he has mastered it.
Children learn best when we work with them
rather than when we send them off on a solo mission.

BRENDA HUNTER

57.

Any mother who educates her child
brings to the task something no paid educator has to offer.
Not only does she have a stronger emotional investment
in her child, but she works one-on-one.
No teacher can give a child that quality of attention.

58.

Gifted children not only have high IQs,
they also have involved parents
who realize they are their children's first teachers.

59.

When God gives you a dream, he will help you to realize it.
It may take a year or half a lifetime,
but God planted that dream in your consciousness for a reason.
God and you will make dreams become realities.

60.

A baby is a baby only once.
He cannot relive his infancy
any more than you can relive your youth.
Spend the necessary time with him now
so that you will have few regrets later on.

BRENDA HUNTER

61.

Leah Lampone, former Milwaukee County circuit judge,
left the bench after fourteen years to come home
and care for her children. She said,
"Looking back upon my years as both judge and mother,
I have come to realize the greatest impact I have made in any life
is that which I've made in the lives of my children."

62.

We are happiest—gloriously, deeply happy—
when we are giving love to others.

63.
Like children, a husband flourishes
when his needs have a high priority in his wife's life.

64.
Take time to establish eye contact with your husband.
The longer we are married, the more we look away
or down or anywhere but in each other's eyes.
Yet lovers gaze soulfully at each other.

BRENDA HUNTER

65.

When your husband speaks,
listen carefully, without interrupting.
If you listen with your heart, he will love talking to you
and will come to believe he cannot get by
without your wisdom and counsel.

66.

Few things destroy a child's sense of security
more than witnessing ugly marital battles.
It is important that you and your husband keep short lists
and practice self-control.

67.

When you are old, among your treasures
will be the note your eight-year-old wrote you
and the pressed flower she gave you a half-century before.

68.

You can't teach your child to read in an hour
or stretch his mind in a few days.
Your children need your consistent
and patient teaching—over the long haul.
As you invest much time in your children's lives,
the yield will be great.

BRENDA HUNTER

69.

Few children enjoy coming home to an empty house
or staying home alone when they are sick.
At times like these, our kids
need us more than ever—to supervise, care, and listen.

70.

Adolescent girls can be extremely self-centered.
They concentrate on guys, their friends, guys, zits,
guys, shopping, guys, and their hair.
Fortunately, this myopia fades in their twenties.

71.

One wife made her desperate husband a T-shirt
that said on the front: "I survived my wife's menopause."
On the back it read:
"My wife wouldn't take estrogen, so I did."

72.

Spouses who are critical, contemptuous,
and defensive are headed for trouble.
So watch your words, tone of voice,
and tendency to blame or defend.
Most of all, don't withdraw.

BRENDA HUNTER

73.

Our children are not trophies, accessories,
or extracurricular activities to engage in after hours.
They are gifts from God
to be cherished and equipped for life.

74.

If you rear your children well,
when they grow up and leave home,
you will have the deep satisfaction of a job well done
and the inner freedom to turn your attention
to changing your culture.

75.

If you are at war with either of your parents,
your children will suffer. To be at peace with yourself
and bring sufficient emotional energy to mothering,
you need to be at peace with your parents.
Forgive them even if you can't be emotionally close.

76.

If you help a mother love her life,
you will help a family.
And as families go, so goes society.

BRENDA HUNTER

77.

"Among babies, there are no connivers,
con artists, or hypocrites....
Babies are honest:
What you see is what you get."

EVELYN B. THOMAN, PH.D., PSYCHOLOGIST AND AUTHOR OF *BORN DANCING*

78.

Newborns are adept at imitation.
Try making an *o* or sticking out your tongue
the next time you hold a baby.

79.

A mother needs to think of herself as a scientist
and her home as a memory laboratory.
Each happy experience adds to the warm, positive memories
her children will carry through life.

80.

Your children are listening even when they are bored
or have blank looks on their faces.
At these moments when they are most infuriating,
their brains may be hard at work.

BRENDA HUNTER

81.

Celebrate all birthdays at your house.
Write a note to the birthday person,
telling him how much he means to you.
This enhances self-esteem in husbands,
as well as children.

82.

Our children are like sponges. They absorb family rules,
values, and their self-perceptions from us.
They're not mature enough to discriminate the truth
in the messages they receive, so we need to be careful what we say.

83.

Being a mother has taught me to pray.
Many times when my children were in high school
and college I awoke in the middle of the night
and felt I should pray for them.
Later I learned that God
had protected them on numerous occasions.

84.

A mother gives her child a unique gift: a sense of belonging.
Without a mother's devoted love,
a person may feel a little homeless all his life.

BRENDA HUNTER

85.

No matter how clever you think you are,
your kids will outwit you.
I told my girls that they could not kick each other or pull hair,
thinking this would keep fighting to a minimum.
It wasn't long before I found Holly sitting
on her sister's stomach, breathing into her face,
as Kristen's head flipped wildly to and fro, like a dying fish.
Holly had a new weapon: onion breath.

86.

How important is any mother? Ask her child.

87.

One friend says
that when a woman buys new lingerie,
she should get an "anything goes" outfit for those nights away
from the children.

88.

Among the most important skills
you and your husband will ever acquire
are conflict resolution skills.
Both of you need to be winners
at the end of any fight.

BRENDA HUNTER

89.

"Fathers play critical roles for their children as teachers.
They always have. The Greeks, Hebrews, Romans, and,
more recently, Puritans, from whom we inherited our culture,
expected fathers to be the family catechizers
and providers of spiritual and practical training."

KARL ZINSMEISTER, AUTHOR

90.

Once you become a mother,
your husband is the most important support player in your life.
(After that, comes your mother.)

91.

"Fathers, do not exasperate your children;
instead, bring them up in the training and instruction
of the Lord."

EPHESIANS 6:4, NIV

92.

Scientific data now prove that men and women
are wired differently. That means fathers can't be mothers,
and mothers can't be fathers. Children need both.
Our grandmothers knew this instinctively.

BRENDA HUNTER

93.

You need—you deserve—lunch out
with a close female friend once a week.

94.

The practice of hospitality
is not dependent on having the perfect home.
I went to the home of a wealthy friend one day,
and she did not even offer me a cup of coffee.
Later, I visited a friend of limited means,
and she gave me tea, homemade bread, and jam.

95.

You create your own ambiance.
Whether you surround yourself with flowers or clutter,
you control your environment.
If you don't like what you see, change it.

96.

When you are lonely, comfort yourself
with the knowledge that all humans are lonely at times.
Fix yourself a cup of tea,
listen to soothing music, and call a dear friend on the phone.
As you confide in her, your loneliness will subside.

BRENDA HUNTER

97.

All mothers suffer from feelings of guilt
and believe, on occasion,
that they have ruined their children's lives.
It's the persistent guilt that should sound a warning bell.

98.

Unlike a babysitter, a mother knows
she cannot quit and go home at the end of the day.
Her love for her child keeps her giving,
believing, and teaching at all hours.

99.

Your childhood experiences with your mother
directly affect your reservoir of mother love.
Women who were well nurtured find mothering easier
than those who were not. If your maternal well feels empty,
your husband and mother-in-law can help fill it up.

100.

Want to know what your children will remember
about you when they grow up?
Ask them now and learn from their responses.

BRENDA HUNTER

101.

One mother says she needs no scientist to tell her
that boys and girls are different. From birth,
her now two-year-old son has been different from her girls.
"For one thing, my son runs around the house
spitting—at the girls, furniture, and me.
My girls never dreamed of doing that."

102.

"Dear Mommy, I love you so much.
What would I do without you?"
A note from my daughter Kristen, at age 10

103.
A woman *can* have it all,
but not all at once.

104.
Thirty years of research in the social sciences
show that children from intact families
are physically and emotionally healthier
and perform better academically
than children from single or remarried families.
This is even more motivation for us
to make our marriage work.

BRENDA HUNTER

105.
Don't make the refrigerator your friend.
Deal with the real issues,
and then overeating will become less of a problem.

106.
Wives need their husbands' wholehearted support
to be superb mothers. If your husband does not support
your lifestyle choice—whether you work inside
or outside your home—you may have great internal conflict.
You and your husband need to agree on this important issue.

107.

"My education was wholly centered
in the glance, more or less serene,
and the smile, more or less open, of my mother.
The reins of my heart were in her hand."

LAMARTINE, FRENCH POET

108.

As a child
if you were well loved by both parents,
you are among the most fortunate of women,
and you need to tell your parents so.

BRENDA HUNTER

109.

Susanna Wesley, mother of Charles and John,
taught her ten children at home
while running an orderly household.
When each child turned five, she taught him the alphabet,
and then they began reading the Bible,
beginning with Genesis 1:1.

110.

No therapist can reparent an individual as well
as a good mother and father can parent the first time around.

111.

Never underestimate the amount of learning that occurs
when you take your child to the grocery store or park.
Talk to her about her interests,
and use your time together to broaden her knowledge.
As you spend time together in the simple activities of life,
your child is learning, growing, and developing values
through those rich and varied experiences.

112.

Children need time—time to think, to putter,
to hang around their moms and dads.

BRENDA HUNTER

113.

When I was a new mother,
I felt that my children would never grow up.
At the end of a day of changing diapers, attending to cries,
or engaging in baby talk, I wondered if I was teetering
on the brink of mental retardation.
I've learned since that kids do grow up and most leave home.

114.

Comparing your children to each other
increases sibling rivalry. Praise each child for work well done,
and help each develop his potential.

115.

With the help of God,
you can forgive those who have hurt you,
and thereby you will become a better mother to your children.

116.

Home needs to be a safe place.
This does not mean, however, that we should ignore or deny
hurt or angry feelings.
Instead we should speak the truth,
tempered with love and kindness, asking forgiveness
when we wound each other.

BRENDA HUNTER

117.

It's hard to believe, after you've refereed fights,
wiped noses, and answered a zillion questions,
that you've shaped attitudes and lives that day.

118.

"With my mother's death all settled happiness,
all that was tranquil and reliable disappeared from my life.
There was much fun, many pleasures, many stabs of joy;
but no more of the old security. It was sea and islands now;
the great continent had sunk like Atlantis."

C.S. LEWIS, *SURPRISED BY JOY*

119.

When your children become adolescents
and you are premenopausal, your house will rock,
especially if you have more than one adolescent daughter.
As one husband said, "There's never a good week."

120.

Too often, adolescents find the empty house
a convenient place for afternoon sex and drug use.
That's why it's so important to have an adult at home
when they come through the door.

BRENDA HUNTER

121.

School age children need a desk,
a quiet place to study, and enforced study hours.
Even when they become teenagers wired to the phone,
you need to enforce study hours.
They'll thank you later when they reap rewards
from their academic successes.

122.

Teenagers kick against the pricks,
but deep inside they long for parents to be firmly in control.
So continue to hold the line.

123.

If you and your mother live far apart or can't be friends,
find a warm, older woman who will act as a mentor.

124.

When I was a young writer working at home
and filled with self-doubt, I took the well-known writer
Madeleine L'Engle to lunch.
After listening to my struggle to get to the typewriter,
L'Engle said crisply that if I worked more diligently,
I would have less time for self-doubt.
This key bit of mentoring helped shape me as a writer.

BRENDA HUNTER

125.

If your husband felt rejected by his mother as a small boy,
he may fear intimacy with you.
The small boy inside him still needs to learn
that his wife is not aloof and rejecting
like his mother.

126.

A woman needs a man in her life who feels she is *enough*.
She does not need a Pygmalion who tries to change her.
Rather she needs to feel her husband loves her
just as she sits, walks, stands.

127.

One morning a wife heard her husband say he wished they could go to the beach but knew they couldn't afford it. When he came home that night, he heard the Beach Boys on the stereo. His smiling wife led him to the backyard for a picnic on the "beach" she had created by hauling in bags of sand. He was touched that she had "heard" his need.

128.

Your husband's hunger for your affirmation
is as great as his hunger for sex (greater when he hits midlife!).

BRENDA HUNTER

129.

If you wish to have compassionate, responsible,
and moral children,
you must be a compassionate, responsible, and moral parent.
How could it be otherwise?

130.

Remember that the wild two-year-old,
if undisciplined, will become the surly six-year-old.
If left untamed, he may become
the uncontrolled teenager who breaks your heart.
Take charge now.

131.

"Love the LORD your God with all your heart
and with all your soul
and with all your strength.
These commandments that I give you today
are to be upon your hearts.
Impress them on your children.
Talk about them when you sit at home
and when you walk along the road,
when you lie down and when you get up."

DEUTERONOMY 6:5-7, NIV

BRENDA HUNTER

132.

Home is a hospital for flagging self-esteem and wounded spirits.
We bind up our children's wounds
after they return home from the war zone that is school,
and we minister to our husband,
harried by the demands of work.
When we bring lonely or hurting people into our homes,
they leave larger than they came.

133.

"There is no influence so powerful as that of the mother."
SARAH JOSEPHA HALL, AMERICAN PIONEER AND WRITER

134.

Women wither in isolation.
Find or create a group of other like-minded mothers,
and your life will be richer for it.

135.

Don't give in to the blues.
Try to catch yourself on the downhill slide.
Take a walk, have an intimate conversation with a friend,
or finish a project.
If depression lingers, seek professional help.

BRENDA HUNTER

136.

Separation is hard for very young children.
Until your child is nearly two years old, he doesn't have a mental
picture of you to comfort himself in your absence.
So he is anxious when you are gone.

137.

"A young child's hunger for his mother's love and presence
is as great as his hunger for food; and her absence
inevitably generates 'a powerful sense of loss and anger.'"

JOHN BOWLBY, BRITISH PSYCHIATRIST

138.

"You have a wonderful child.
Then, when he's thirteen, gremlins carry him away
and leave in his place a stranger
who gives you not a moment's peace."

JILL EIKENBERRY, ACTRESS

139.

If parents are warm, loving, and available,
a child comes to believe that he is lovable and worthy.
If parents are cold and rejecting or too busy,
then the child is likely to feel unloved and unworthy.

BRENDA HUNTER

140.

Children always want their parents in the audience,
no matter how insignificant their role in the play.
And if they finish at the back of the pack,
make sure you are there to cheer them on.

141.

Attend that first PTA meeting in the fall.
Teachers form impressions about your interest in your child
and his schooling partially based on your attendance
at school functions.

142.

The chief problem with contemporary feminism
is that it fails to address a woman's deep
and abiding desire to nurture her children.
Nor does it recognize the enormous fulfillment
marriage can render.

143.

Juggling a variety of roles may seem like a good idea,
but some balls—like family, marriage, and children—
are more fragile than others.

BRENDA HUNTER

144.

Don't base your identity exclusively on what you *do*.
Instead, understand that you are more
than your varied roles of wife, mother, worker.
You are you. Focus on *being*.

145.

We need to take time to live a life.
If we are hurtling through space, always over extended,
having little time for intimacy,
we need to ask ourselves: What deep hole am I trying to fill?
Whose love am I trying to win?

146.

All women get depressed at times,
whether they are employed at home or in the workplace.
In fact, women are twice as likely as men
to struggle with depression.

147.

Most of us reject a part of ourselves:
our hair, our breasts, our thighs.
Happily, when we reach our forties and fifties,
we learn to become more accepting of our bodies.

BRENDA HUNTER

148.

Many men suffer from father hunger. If they weren't
emotionally close to their dads, they parent in a vacuum.
Men need—at any age—a positive, affirming relationship
with a wise, older man.

149.

Throughout your life span you will have more friends
than your husband, but you need to encourage him to reach out
and form friendships with other men.
He will tend to rely heavily on you to meet his emotional needs,
but friendships will enrich his life.

150.

Whether a mother works inside or outside her home,
she invariably carries the burden
for the psychological welfare of her children.
That's why we worry more about our kids than our husbands do.

151.

"We cannot insist
that the first years of infancy are of supreme importance,
and that mothers are not of supreme importance."

G. K. CHESTERTON, BRITISH AUTHOR

BRENDA HUNTER

152.

You and your daughter
have the most complex relationship within your family.
Research shows that you will be a major player in her life
her whole life long.

153.

Tell your daughter never to marry a man
who makes her feel *less than*.
Tell her to wait for the man who makes her feel
she can climb mountains, ford rivers, or change the world.

154.

"I look back on my life like a good day's work;
it was done and I feel satisfied with it.
I was happy and contented…and life is what we make it,
always has been, always will be."

GRANDMA MOSES, ARTIST AND MOTHER OF TEN

155.

If you choose to take a season of your life
to devote to your family, be wholehearted about your choice.
Otherwise, you will miss the best that this season has to offer.

BRENDA HUNTER

156.

Studies show that people obtain higher scores
on intelligence tests in their fifties than in their twenties.
Most studies, in fact, show no decline in mental capacity
until age seventy! As we grow older, we have better ways
of organizing knowledge and solving problems
than when we were younger.

157.

You are of great worth, whether you feel like it or not.
God created you, and you have something unique
to give the world. If you fail to use your gifts,
God will still love you, but the world will be a poorer place.

158.

Ideas have consequences.
In the 1980s the idea that anyone could care for children
as well as mother herself held sway. In the 1990s
two new myths have emerged: that kids are infinitely resilient
and that fathers are unnecessary.

159.

Warm, nurturing dads are critical in teaching their sons values.
According to Bill Glass, former professional football player
who has worked for years with prisoners,
"I've never met an inmate who loves his dad."

BRENDA HUNTER

160.

Spend ten minutes each day alone with each child.
This not only increases the child's self-esteem
and protects his mental health,
but it cuts down on sibling rivalry as well.

161.

You are the "secure base" for your children as long as you live.
They will leave home and return to you throughout their lives,
drawing strength from your love and presence.

162.

It's a mistake to push babies and toddlers
into independence too early. If we allow our children
to be dependent when they are young,
they will become happily independent as they mature.

163.

If you want your child to become an achiever,
you need to be his safety net.
With your love undergirding him, he can take risks,
knowing you will be there if he falls.

BRENDA HUNTER

164.

Baroness Jane von Lawick-Goodall,
who spent years studying chimpanzee behavior,
modeled her mothering after the mothering she had observed
among the chimpanzees. She never left her son screaming,
and she kept him with her when he was young.
The result? He "felt secure from the beginning."

165.

"A woman's whole life is a history of the affections."

WASHINGTON IRVING

166.

Family rituals strengthen your child's self-esteem.
Birthday celebrations, nightly family dinners,
and visits to the relatives—all are important.

167.

Quality time is rooted in the soil of quantity time.
Only as you spend quantity time with your children
can you have any guarantee that you will be around
for those golden moments of quality time.

BRENDA HUNTER

168.

One friend keeps romance alive with a secret code.
In the morning she spreads her prettiest nightgown across the bed
to signal her intentions for the evening ahead.
She says her husband always comes to breakfast smiling.

169.

Even in the midst of your children's ever-present,
clamoring needs, make your husband a top priority,
or what's a marriage for?

170.

In all marriages adults feel and express anger.
But in happy marriages positive comments and actions
greatly outweigh the negative.

171.

A friend said that once when he returned home
from a business trip, flung open the door,
and discovered his wife wasn't home,
it was as if their home were devoid of light.
All warmth was centered in Katie's smile.

BRENDA HUNTER

172.

You cannot become a father to your children
if you lose your husband to death, divorce, or workaholism.
Nor should you try.
It is important, however, to have attentive, warm men
in their lives—grandfathers, uncles, coaches, teachers—who can
fill that void.

173.

Fathers are critical in their children's sex role development.
Studies show that dads, not moms, teach little boys to become
men and young girls to become women.

174.

Daughters love to go out to lunch or tea with mom.
Sons like to hang around the kitchen and talk.
It's important that you make time in your life for these outings
and everyday moments.

175.

To imply that mother care is the same as other care
is to say there is nothing unique
about the mother-child relationship.
Who really believes that?

BRENDA HUNTER

176.

Mothers who spend quality and quantity time
with their kids have children who are better adjusted,
more motivated to learn, and capable of higher achievement.

177.

Reading aloud to your children from birth
is an excellent way to build vocabulary, instill a love for books,
and create lifelong reading habits.

178.

Ask your child's teacher to come for tea or dinner.
This helps the teacher get to know you and your child better
and builds a bond. Then you have an ally in helping
your child succeed at school.

179.

Our children are not infinitely resilient.
Their emotional development is more vulnerable to their
environment than their intellectual development is.

BRENDA HUNTER

180.

No one will ever love your child
as passionately over the long haul as you and your husband.
And your child needs that "crazy about you" love
to believe in himself.

181.

Kids often turn to sex because of a lack of love at home.
If you wish to inoculate your teenagers against premarital sex,
tell them you disapprove, but also give them lots of warm,
appropriate affection. A mom's disapproval of premarital sex
is a powerful deterrent, especially for daughters.

182.

If you don't teach your son to be sexually moral,
he may deeply regret his past when he finally falls in love
with a woman worthy of his respect.
And she may feel lonely on their wedding night
when what is new for her is familiar for him.
Promiscuity ultimately wounds the person one loves the most.

183.

Teach your adolescent sons and daughters to guard their hearts.
Just as their lives reflect character and integrity,
they deserve these qualities in a mate.

BRENDA HUNTER

184.

Sometimes as mothers we are startled
by what our children learn from their peers.
Five-year-old Madeleine had just started kindergarten.
As she and her mother pulled out of McDonald's,
Madeleine said innocently, "Let's get the hell outa here."

185.

Studies show that babies who have secure emotional bonds
to their parents tend to become cooperative preschoolers
and kindergartners. They also possess more coping skills
than their insecure counterparts.

186.

When we give our very young children to others to rear,
what is at issue is not only their emotional bond with us
but also our power to influence them later on.
That's a lot to put at risk for any reason.

187.

Your children have an innate innocence that needs to be
protected. Young children do not need to know what we adults
know about sex. They need to be able to experience childhood,
while having us answer their questions about sex accurately
and in age-appropriate ways.

BRENDA HUNTER

188.

Baby boomers who experimented with drugs and sex
often have difficulty asking their own children to abstain.
What can a parent do? Be honest about what you did wrong,
teach abstinence, and let your children know
you want to spare them the pain.

189.

Write a letter to your child and tell her
why she is valuable to you. Then ask her to write to you,
telling you about the happy moments in her childhood.
You can build on these powerful, positive memories.

190.

For every negative comment you make to your mate,
you will need to speak three or four positives
just to get back to square one.

191.

Our husbands are often our mentors.
My husband is mine. His favorite word is "productive."
I owe many of my accomplishments to this man
who believes I can do any "productive" thing I set my mind to.

BRENDA HUNTER

192.

Those who create happy marriages usually come
from families where the parents were happily married.
Marital happiness tends to run in families.

193.

New brain research indicates that men have greater spatial abilities
and women have greater language facility.
That's why we are better at arguing than our husbands.

194.

Although you may feel that your brain is atrophying
as you age, psychologists tell us that if we use our brain power
we won't lose it. So build intellectually stimulating activities
into your life.

195.

What are you living for? Money? Career?
The beautiful home and perfect family?
It is essential to have a higher purpose, one that can shape
your life in a positive, altruistic direction.

BRENDA HUNTER

196.

We need to discover and value our gifts, whatever they are.
I once asked an admiral's wife what she enjoyed doing,
and she said, "Silly little things, like needlepoint and gardening."
I felt sad that this gracious woman saw no value in those
activities that gave her pleasure. All our gifts enrich our world.

197.

I once interviewed an eighty-five-year-old who looked sixty-five.
When I asked her the secret of her youth and vitality,
she said, "I've always loved life, and I've tried to learn something
new every day."

198.

You are not just diapering and feeding your baby.
You are teaching him lessons about love and intimacy
that will last a lifetime.

199.

You're not only rearing your own children,
you are influencing future generations.
Your influence will be felt in your larger family
long after your name has been forgotten.

BRENDA HUNTER

200.

If you punish your children for being honest,
they may become liars.
Tell them that they are courageous when they tell the truth.
Then quietly and deliberately walk them
through the consequences of their actions.

201.

Your children will feel like failures at times,
so you need to help them believe in themselves again and again.
Maximize their strengths and speak sparingly of their weaknesses.

202.

"Children are most like us in their feelings
and least like us in their thoughts."

DR. DAVID ELKIND, CHILD PSYCHOLOGIST

203.

If you harp on your child's weaknesses,
she may become hurt, sullen, and angry.
With your patient love and training, some of her
weaknesses may become her greatest strengths.

BRENDA HUNTER

204.

Our culture is enamored of intellectual development,
but people can be intellectual giants and emotional pygmies.
Emotional development in children
is foundational for intellectual development.

205.

At heart, every undisciplined child feels unloved.
If you want your child to understand that you care about him,
you must shape his behavior. Be firm, but not harsh.

206.

After one mother explained to her six-year-old daughter that Jesus could come into her heart, the girl smiled serenely and said, "Mommy, I know that Jesus is in my heart because I can feel his head in my tummy."

207.

As a psychologist, I believe children could care less about designer clothes, prep schools, fancy vacations, and endless gadgets. They want our love spelled TIME.

BRENDA HUNTER

208.

Don't forget that you are more than your husband's wife.
You are his lover and his best friend, too.

209.

Be a diligent steward of the money you and your husband earn.
Try to avoid impulsive spending, and keep credit card debt
at a minimum. Give back to God a portion of all he gives to you.
My husband and I have never had serious financial problems
since we began to tithe.

210.

When money is tight, buy bread,
but don't forget to purchase hyacinths for the soul.

211.

Learn to say no to excessive demands by schools,
volunteer groups, and churches.
As parents of young children, you and your husband
need to channel your energies into your family.
Give those in midlife a chance to serve.

BRENDA HUNTER

212.

Helen Jackson gave up the opportunity to become the first black astronaut because a son was floundering. In an interview, a Canadian talk show host asked if she had any regrets. "No," said Helen, "I would have liked to be an astronaut, but my children needed me at home, and their needs came first."

213.

Live in such a way that you will never say, "I wish I had spent more time getting to know my children."

214.

Modern women may have been liberated,
but their babies haven't been.
Babies' needs remain the same,
no matter what lifestyle their mothers choose.

215.

Child development experts agree that all babies need sensitive,
consistent, and responsive mothering.
A mother needs to pick up on her baby's signals consistently
and respond lovingly and sensitively most of the time.

BRENDA HUNTER

216.

Happy is the man who was well loved by his father
and happy his children after him.
This father's good parenting will be a legacy
for many generations to follow.

217.

"We are moulded and remoulded by those who have loved us;
and though the love may pass,
we are nevertheless their work, for good or ill."

FRANCOIS MAURIAC, FRENCH NOBEL LAUREATE

218.

When you are lost in a struggle,
find a friend who's struggling too and comfort her.
When we give comfort, often it comes back to us immediately.

219.

We can have rich productive lives in midlife and beyond.
In their forties, Harriet Beecher Stowe wrote *Uncle Tom's Cabin*
and Madeleine L'Engle won an award for *A Wrinkle in Time.*
And Margaret Craven published her first novel,
I Heard the Owl Call My Name, at the age of sixty-nine.

BRENDA HUNTER

220.

If we felt rejected by our fathers in childhood,
we may find it hard to invest in motherhood.
Instead, we may become avid careerists—hoping to capture
the elusive brass ring—our fathers' approval.

221.

It's cheaper to work from home.
You save on commuting costs, expensive lunches out,
and child care expenses. That's why myriad women are trading
business suits for jeans and working from home.
Besides, home is where the kids are.

222.

What helps our children say no to drugs?
Their emotionally close relationship with their parents.
Harvard psychiatrist Armand Nicholi says that teens
turn to drugs because they feel lonely and isolated
and suffer from "a moral and spiritual void."
Our teenagers need someone at home to talk to,
someone to monitor their after-school activities.

223.

It is possible for a mother to give her child
more than she received growing up—more time, more love,
more attention.

BRENDA HUNTER

224.

If we base our identity chiefly on what we *do*,
how will we handle those times in life when we are sick or old
and can do very little?

225.

What's your passion?
What, besides your family, consumes your thought and attention?
Even when you have toddlers, you can read, learn,
and become involved on a manageable scale, as you prepare
for the time when you can make a difference in society.

226.

"In the next year or so my signature will appear on $60 billion of United States currency. More important to me, however, is the signature that appears on my life—the strong, proud, assertive handwriting of a loving father and mother."

KATHERINE D. ORTEGA, FORMER TREASURER OF THE U.S.

227.

Teach your children about God when they are young and impressionable. This will enable them to grow up feeling that they are not alone in the universe, and their lives will never lack a moral compass.

BRENDA HUNTER

228.
There are no perfect parents.
We did not have them; we will not be them.
But if we received a legacy of love and positive self-regard
from our parents, we will find parenting easier.

229.
Being a mother has turned me inside out.
I am not the same woman I was twenty-six years ago.
I have been stretched by my children in ways
I could not have imagined, but I am the better for it.

230.

According to the Family Research Council,
a Washington, D.C. think tank, American children are starving
for parental time. The amount of time families spend together
has declined 40 percent in the past twenty-five years.

231.

The first ten minutes after your children come home
from school are golden. During these brief moments,
they are most eager to share the highs and lows of their day.
After this time passes, the excitement wanes,
and they are on to other things.

BRENDA HUNTER

232.

Increasingly, educators are seeing younger and younger kids
commit wrong without remorse.
How does a child develop a conscience?
First, he needs a strong emotional tie with his mother and father.
Then, because he loves his parents and wants to please them,
he absorbs their messages about right and wrong.

233.

Psychologists have found that fathers forge emotional bonds
with their children through play, mothers through nurturing.

234.

"I grow lives.
Sometimes as a writer; always as a mother.
And I grow my own."

SHERRY VON OHLSEN

235.

Few child development experts understand children
as well as the average mom.
Experts study children as objects of scientific research.
Moms *know* kids and their habits, inside and out.

BRENDA HUNTER

236.

If your child is having trouble at school,
don't blame his teacher. Schedule an appointment,
dress your best, and go with the express purpose
of enlisting the teacher's help in turning your child
into a winner. It's too easy to blame others.
We need to look for causes within our own homes.

237.

"In automobile terms, the child supplies the power
but the parents have to do the steering."

BENJAMIN SPOCK, *BABY AND CHILD CARE*

238.

If you do not teach your child to be true,
courageous, disciplined, and God-fearing, who will?
When hard times come—and they must—only what is inside
your child will help him endure.

239.

If we want our children to become disciplined,
responsible adults, we need to teach them to work.
Even a toddler can empty wastebaskets,
and a twelve-year-old can help paint a room.
Don't let a week go by without teaching your child
how to work at a task with you.

BRENDA HUNTER

240.

A daughter who feels that her father adores her
(and really loves her mother)
will be supremely confident with men in adulthood.

241.

Studies show that males are more vulnerable to malnutrition,
schizophrenia, delinquency, academic underachievement,
and suicide than females are. Until they reach adulthood,
your sons will need more from you than they ask for—
more reassurance, more love, more time, more supervision.

242.

Unrealistic expectations trap our kids in a web of failure.
Few things hurt more than being unable to please one's parents.

243.

Eminent child psychiatrist E. James Anthony
has said that self-esteem drops precipitously at age twelve
and climbs thereafter.
That's why your junior high child is so obnoxious and needy.
What can you do? Listen. Stay involved.
Laugh as much as you can.

BRENDA HUNTER

244.

"You don't raise heroes, you raise sons.
And if you treat them like sons, they'll turn out to be heroes,
even if it's just in your own eyes."

WALTER M. SCHIRRA, SR.

245.

A mother of an all-American wrestler said,
"When I see my son on the mat, I know I helped him get there.
I'm in the stands cheering for him (and giving
my ear-piercing whistle) but, most importantly,
I've been cheering for him all his life."

246.

Dads are critical in child development. When boys grow up
without dads, they may become prone to violence.
Over 70 percent of juveniles in long-term correctional
facilities grew up without fathers.

DAVID BLANKENHORN, PRESIDENT OF THE INSTITUTE FOR AMERICAN VALUES

247.

"Women as the guardians of children possess great power.
They are the molders of their children's personality
and the arbiters of their development."

ANN OAKLEY, ENGLISH SOCIOLOGIST

BRENDA HUNTER

248.

The most critical voice we will ever hear
is inside our own heads. We need to turn down the volume
or, still better, switch it off.

249.

Whether she is a potter, karate champ, aerobics fanatic,
neighborhood psychologist, or budding politician,
the mother at home has the opportunity to expand her horizons,
to take a talent and run with it.

250.

If we feel trapped financially, we need to ask ourselves:
Is it need or greed? We Americans see conspicuous consumption
as a necessity, not a luxury.

251.

I tell my daughters that when they marry,
it's a good idea to live on their husband's income,
banking theirs or using some of it for extras.
That way they won't count on their income for the mortgage.
This will give them the freedom to take time out
for their children if they so choose.

BRENDA HUNTER

252.

God could not be everywhere and therefore he made mothers.

JEWISH PROVERB

253.

Psychologist Evelyn Thoman says that babies "dance"
in synchrony to their mother's speech.
Watch to see if your baby extends an elbow, rotates
a shoulder or makes a circle with a big toe as you speak.

254.

Genius is seldom the product of an overscheduled life.
Genius needs fallow time to flourish.

255.

C.S. Lewis and his brother spent countless hours as children
in their attic writing stories. As an adult,
Lewis wrote his now-classic Narnia tales for children.
Our children need time and opportunities
to use their imaginations and to be creative.

BRENDA HUNTER

256.

Expose your child to museums, theater, and new experiences.
If you can afford it, give him lessons.
But don't expect him to become a world-class pianist
or famous actor so that you can feel like a good mother.
Work on your own achievements.

257.

When our children are young,
it is not always possible to gauge the impact
we are having in their lives.
We have to walk in faith.

258.

In *Finding Herself* psychologist Ruth Josselson says
that women anchor their lives in relationships
while men competitively strive for separateness.

259.

For a man to feel emotionally secure in his marriage,
his wife needs to be positive and accepting most of the time.
Then he can dare to be vulnerable
and share his deepest thoughts and feelings.

BRENDA HUNTER

260.

A producer on a national talk show predicted
that the hot issue of the nineties would be how best
to rear America's children. We who value mothering
need to become an unstoppable force in a culture
that devalues children.

261.

Every child's birthright is "good enough" mothering.

262.

"Your baby comes into this world
biologically designed to respond to others' feelings.
Babies only a few hours old will often start wailing
when they hear another newborn cry."

EVELYN B. THOMAN, PSYCHOLOGIST AND AUTHOR OF *BORN DANCING*

263.

Psychologists Mary Ainsworth and Sylvia Bell
found that when mothers respond with sensitivity
to their babies' cries in the first three months of life,
the babies tend to cry less later on.

BRENDA HUNTER

264.

The young child's relationship with his mother
is "unique, without parallel, established unalterably
for a whole lifetime as the first and strongest love object
and as the prototype of all later love relationships for both sexes."

SIGMUND FREUD

265.

"Children are the anchors that hold a mother to life."

SOPHOCLES

266.

As parents, we need to be aware of our children's unique gifts.
One child may possess academic intelligence
and another, social intelligence. Another may be a fine athlete.
We must not try to have cookie cutter children.
Instead, we can help each identify and achieve his potential.

267.

Don't push your child into independence too early.
Paradoxically, when he knows he has someone to rely on,
he will become more self-reliant, better able to cope,
and more motivated to be successful.

BRENDA HUNTER

268.

A junior high counselor once told me she had a box of tissues in her office for those kids who couldn't talk to their parents. "It's far better," she said, "for them to talk to their parents than to come to me as a last resort."

269.

What are you doing to stay aware of the incredible pressure your teens face daily? Do you ask them what they're feeling? Are you aware of the choices they're making in the sexual area? Don't be afraid. Ask, and then listen carefully to what they say.

270.

If you don't like your life, have the courage to change it.

271.

If you are a mother at home, map out your week
at its beginning, including some time in the world at large.
Too much time at home will make you stale. Go for a walk,
spend time with a friend, go to the library,
join a coalition of mothers at home and take the kids with you.

BRENDA HUNTER

272.

"Children learn early in life that life is either a gift to be enjoyed or a burden to be borne."

JOHN BOWLBY, BRITISH PSYCHIATRIST

273.

If your child is often angry, this is a sign that something is wrong. Is he getting enough time and attention from you and your husband? Does he feel loved and listened to? Discover what is going on in his heart and his head.

274.
Dreams don't always die;
sometimes they just disappear for a while
to resurface at a better time.

275.
Make your home your laboratory, your office, your studio.
Laura Ashley started her business in her basement flat,
and now her family has shops in London, Tokyo, Melbourne,
Milan, and other cities across the world.

BRENDA HUNTER

276.

Whatever atmosphere we experienced in our home as children—
either warmth and safety or a war zone—is the same atmosphere
we tend to recreate for our children.

277.

We are only together for a season.
Our children will grow up, and then the house will become quiet.
Since our time with them is brief,
let's make the most of the summer of child rearing.
Then we can dance into a winter of rich reward,
rather than shuffle into a season of regret.

278.

"If a child is to keep alive his inborn sense of wonder,
he needs the companionship of at least one adult
who can share it, rediscovering with him the joy,
excitement and mystery of the world we live in."

RACHEL CARSON, AUTHOR OF *THE SENSE OF WONDER*

279.

Intelligence alone does not guarantee academic success.
Some students with average intelligence perform at high levels
while geniuses fail. The most powerful motivator for a child
is time spent with a parent.

BRENDA HUNTER

280.

Most women can make it through the early "boot camp
of motherhood" if they feel that what they're doing
in the daily grind has meaning and purpose.

281.

Now my daughters are grown.
They have become people I like and enjoy.
We often go out for coffee or sit around the dining room table,
talking about literature, current events, life.
Watching them become strong, compassionate women
has given me an enormous sense of fulfillment.

282.

Having taught passive, unimaginative high school students earlier,
I suggested to my husband when our girls were young
that we sell our television and nightly read aloud as a family.
What wonderful times those were!
Over the years we read great books, sitting close,
four abreast on the sofa.

283.

If we are our kids' cheerleaders when they are growing up,
then when we hit midlife, they will become our most ardent
and vocal fans.

BRENDA HUNTER

284.

Parents who are close to their teenagers have been emotionally
close to their kids since they were very young.
It is hard for a parent to suddenly establish intimacy
with a child if he has not put time and effort into developing
a strong relationship throughout that child's life.

285.

Children flourish when parents are warm,
communicative, and firm. Rigid, authoritarian parents
produce children with low self-esteem.
Permissive parents raise children who lack self-discipline.

286.

"To maintain a joyful family requires much from both the parents and children. Each member of the family has to become, in a special way, the servant of the others."

POPE JOHN PAUL II

287.

Try to respond promptly to your children's emotional needs. Don't ask them to put their emotions on ice. Sometimes you may have to push work deadlines ahead to be available, but it's worth it. They will grow up feeling they can trust you and knowing you've always been there for them.

BRENDA HUNTER

288.

Children are born programmed to fall in love with their mothers,
but if their mothers are physically and emotionally absent,
they will fall in love with whomever she has left in charge.

289.

Home can become a place of healing,
even for a mother who was neglected as a child.
As she cares for her own children,
something inside her will go quiet.

290.

Forgiveness is essential to a happy marriage.
We forgive the big wrongs and the little injuries.
Love means having to say you're sorry, again and again.

291.

"Our early lessons in love and our developmental history
shape the expectations we bring into marriage."
JUDITH VIORST, AUTHOR OF *NECESSARY LOSSES*

292.

A woman needs a mentor—someone she admires
about fifteen to twenty years older who is already
well up the mountain she intends to climb,
someone who will say to her,
"Come on up. The air is wonderful up here."

293.

If our bodies are home but our hearts are elsewhere,
even our young children will sense this.
When they grow up, they too may feel that home
is not a good place to be.

294.

"Loving a child doesn't mean giving in to all his whims:
to love him is to bring out the best in him,
to teach him to love what is difficult."

NADIA BOULANGER, FRENCH MUSICIAN AND TEACHER

295.

A violent home is the breeding ground for loneliness
and depression in children.

296.

Play is the work of childhood. Children need time to play
for uninterrupted minutes or hours on end.
As they play imaginatively and cooperatively with peers,
they are working out frustrations and expressing their emotions.

297.

Summer is a magic time—a time for you to throttle back
and enjoy your school age children,
and a time for them to be unhurried and to read, read, read.

298.

"What the mother sings to the cradle
goes all the way down to the coffin."

HENRY WARD BEECHER

299.

When my daughter Holly was a freshman at Columbia
University, she wrote me a beautiful letter for my birthday,
telling me what I meant to her. She thanked me
for my faith in her, for helping her through crises,
for being here. That letter is part of a small collection of treasures
that I would take with me if my house ever caught fire.

BRENDA HUNTER

300.

"The most important person on earth is a mother.
She cannot claim the honor
of having built Notre Dame cathedral.
She need not.
She has built something more magnificent than any cathedral—
a dwelling for an immortal soul,
the tiny perfection of her baby's body."

JOSEPH MINDSZENTY, HUNGARIAN CARDINAL

Finally, a "Sweet Farewell"

My friend Eleanor shared a vignette with me that I'd like to share with you at the close of this book. All the research in the world can hardly improve on this wisdom for wives and mothers.

Eleanor's parents, Bill and Ilde, had a long and happy marriage. An essential ingredient was that they spoke kindly to each other daily but especially in parting. Ilde loved that old hymn whose words were "…and life most sweet as heart to heart speaks kindly when we meet and part."

BRENDA HUNTER

Long after the children were grown, Bill had a heart attack and recovered at home. Ilde, who had gone back to work after the children were grown, came home for lunch each day. One day before she rushed back to work, she hesitated at the door, turned, and said, "I love you, Bill," blowing him a kiss.

Coming home that afternoon she entered their bedroom and discovered that Bill had died. He was looking toward the door, awaiting her return. What a comfort it was to Ilde to know that on their final day together her parting words were sweet and she had said her final good-bye.